STRINGSTASTIC
Level 1
VIOLIN

By Lorraine Chai

2nd Edition

STRINGSTASTIC

PO BOX 815 Epping NSW 1710 Australia
www.stringstastic.com
Copyright © 2017 Lorraine Chai
First Published 2017
2nd Edition 2020
USA Edition 2021

Book design by Meilisa Lengkong

All rights reserved.
Reproduction in whole or in part for any use whatsoever is strictly prohibited.

THE AUTHOR
LORRAINE CHAI

Lorraine is a multi talented instrumentalist and an international educator. She graduated from the Sydney Conservatorium of Music with a Bachelor of Music Studies in 2008 and completed her Graduate Diploma of Education at the Australian Catholic University a year later.

Having grown up with a musical family, Lorraine began piano lessons at the age of four and violin at the age of six, giving her first violin performance at just seven years of age. Lorraine started teaching violin at the age of 14 and founded a string ensemble at her local church. From there, teaching and performing became her passion.

Lorraine loves finding new and exciting ways students can learn their instrument in a classroom setting as well as in private lessons. Along her musical journey and exposure to the various educational methods including Kodaly, Suzuki, Orff, and Dalcroze, Lorraine has also attended Alexander Technique workshops, and has found that she can integrate these various methods into her own teaching technique for the benefit of her students.

Lorraine has extensive ensemble and orchestral experience in Malaysia and in Australia. Lorraine currently the Music Director of Stringstastic Pty Ltd and is an active member with the Australian Strings Association, AUSTA NSW. She also co-ordinates instrumental programmes and runs string ensembles for some of Sydney's most celebrated schools.

PREFACE

This Stringstastic violin book series is specifically designed for beginner violinist aged 6-12 years. Stringstastic Level 1 for violin players introduces young players to the world of violin playing and music theory through games and fun graphics to assist the young violinists better understand the instrument and to learn music theory in an enjoyable way.
This Stringstastic series can be used in a private lesson or along side the viola and cello book series in a classroom setting.

For extra resources, go to www.stringstastic.com to download them for free.

Have fun!!

ACKNOWLEDGEMENT

This book was made possible with the encouragement of my family and loved ones. I would like to thank the following for their advice and input in making this book possible.

Dr. Rita Crews OAM, FMusA (honoris causa), PhD(UNE), BA(Hons), AMusTCL, GradCertDistEd (UNE), FMusicolASMC, HonFNMSM, DipMus (honoris causa) (AICM) MIMT, MACE, MMTA, JP.

Dr. Anthony Clarke DMA, MMus, Grad Dip, BMus Ed, DSCM, FTCL, LMusA, AMusA

CONTENTS

4	STRING FAMILY
5	THE VIOLIN PARTS
7	SIMON SAYS
8	TWO WAYS OF
9	MUSIC STAVE (STAFF)
11	TREBLE CLEF
13	VIOLIN STRINGS
14	BAR LINES
15	READING NOTES
20	POSITION OF STEMS
23	NOTE VALUES
27	WHAT HAVE WE LEARNED SO FAR?
29	RESTS
31	TIME SIGNATURE
33	REVISION
35	ACCIDENTALS
38	D STRING
40	STRINGS AND NOTE NAMES
41	A STRING
43	REVISION D AND A STRING
45	G STRING
47	E STRING
49	REVISION (ON ALL STRINGS)
51	TEST

STRINGSTASTIC

String Family

Which is the smallest string instrument?

Which is the biggest string instrument?

Which instrument do you play?

Suzie and Tommy play in a string quartet. Suzie plays the smallest instrument while Tommy sits down playing his instrument.
Which instruments do Suzie and Tommy play?

Suzie:

Tommy:

Colour in Suzie and Tommy....

The Violin Parts

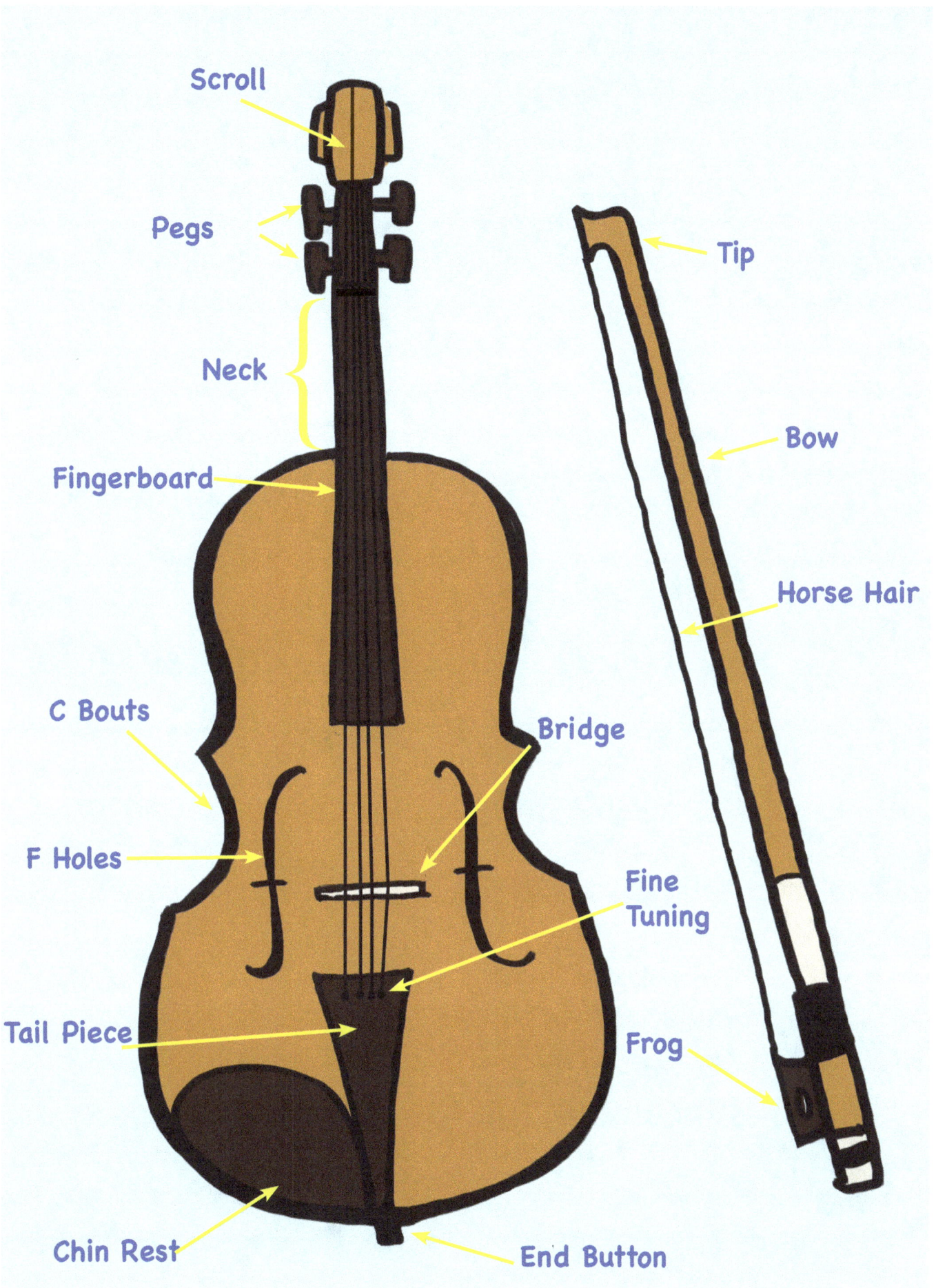

Draw a violin and bow and label their parts.

Simon Says

Your teacher will give you the instructions. You are only allowed to move 5 times in this game. See how many movements you have made by the end of it.

Standing

Imagine you are a ballerina standing nice and tall with your feet in first position.
(Left foot facing the music stand and right foot slightly behind, facing the right corner of music stand.)

Feet together   Your body facing the music stand

Draw your feet on a big piece of paper to remind you of how your feet should look.

Playing Position

Placing the violin up, ready to play

1. Hold the neck of the violin with your left hand and support the violin with your right hand around the right shoulder of the violin. (strings facing you)
2. Rock the violin like a baby and gently swing it up to your left shoulder. (DON'T MOVE YOUR HEAD)
3. Make sure that the violin scroll is at nose level – facing the corner of the music stand.
4. Lastly, rest your chin on the chin rest like you are leaning on a pillow.

How many moves did you make? _____
See if you can remember these directions without looking at the instructions.

Now let us see if you can teach mum or dad how to hold up the violin. How many movements did they make?

Two Ways of...

...holding the violin

RESTING POSITION	PLAYING POSITION
• Hold the violin by the upper part of the C bout with the left hand. • Place the violin under your right armpit with the strings facing outwards *(as shown in the picture)*. • Hug the violin by placing your right fingers on the upper part of the C bout.	• Place the instrument on your left shoulder with your left hand. • Place the left side of your jaw bone on the chin rest. • Hold the violin at shoulder level.

...playing the violin

	MEANING	
arco	Pulling/pushing the bow across the string	
pizzicato or pizz	Plucking the string	

Music Stave (Staff)

Music is written on these lines and spaces below.

 This is called a stave

Trace each line with the different colours and number each line from the bottom up.

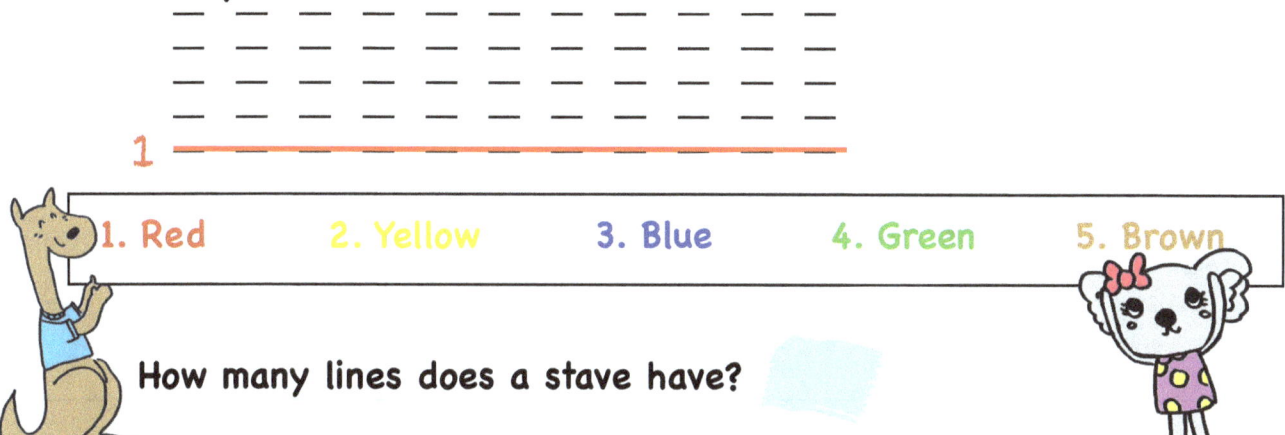

1. Red   2. Yellow   3. Blue   4. Green   5. Brown

How many lines does a stave have?

Draw a note on each line.

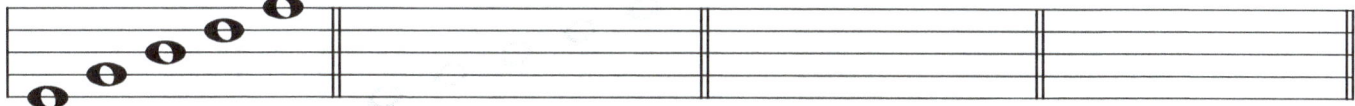

Colour each space with different colours and number each space from the bottom up.

How many spaces does a stave have?

Draw a note in every space.

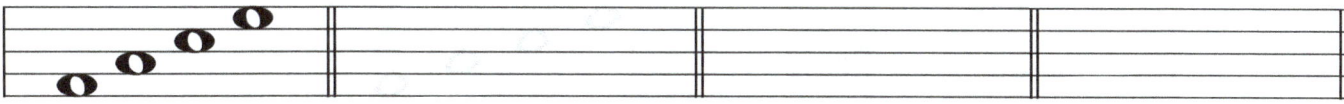

In the stave below, write an L below each note through a line and an S below each note in the spaces.

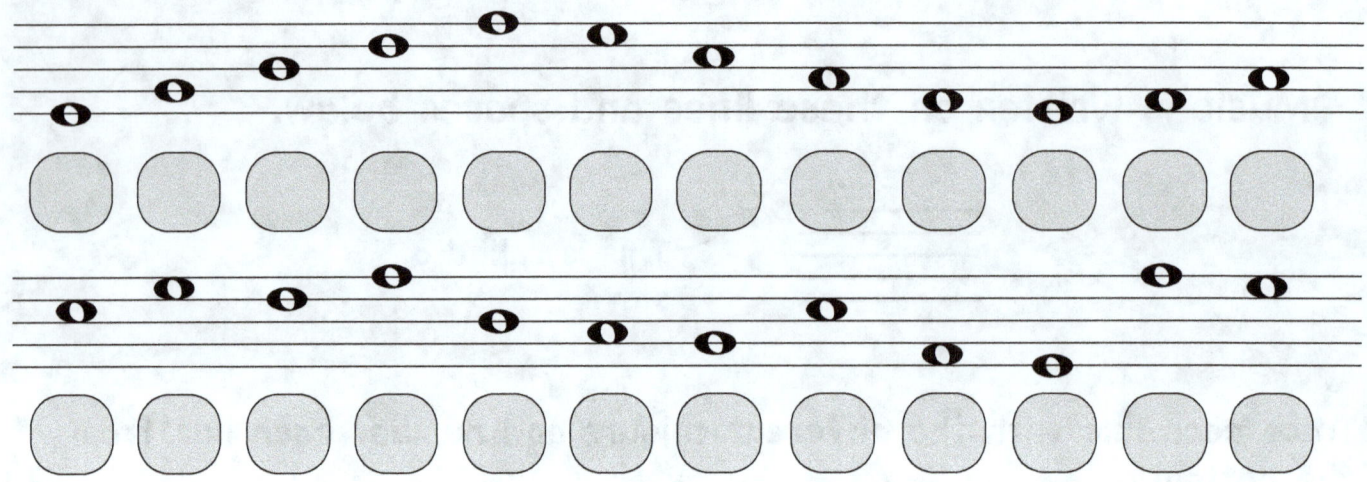

Help Suzie the Koala find her collection of shells.
Colour the shells accordingly.

Shells through the lines red   Shells in the space green

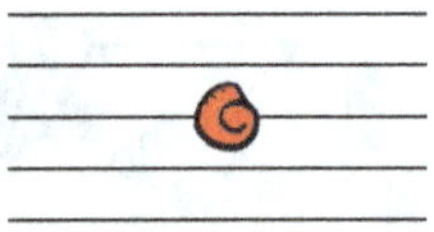

How many shells can you find?

Treble Clef

Music written for the violin uses the Treble Clef only.

A treble clef looks like a person. It has a big body, a small head which is supported by a straight back and the leg hanging down.

Let us practise drawing our treble clefs on this page before we practise drawing them on the stave.

When drawing a treble clef, it must always be a smooth, flowing line starting from the inside out.

Now let us trace these treble clefs and then draw 2 more of your own.

start on the 2nd line where the red dot is

the body of the clef fills up the bottom 2 spaces

the head of the clef goes slightly over the stave so that the head of the clef can breathe and see. Remember to have a straight back through the middle of the body to hold up the clef.

end the clef with a curve hook to the left under the stave so that the clef can stand

Violin Strings

Let's try and remember the names of the open strings.

(Open strings = name of each string without placing any fingers on it)

 G   D   A   E

Greedy   Dinosaurs   Always   Eat

This sentence is called an acronym and helps you remember the names.

(the extra lines above and below the stave are called ledger/leger lines)

Make up your own acronym.

G_____   D_____   A_____   E_____

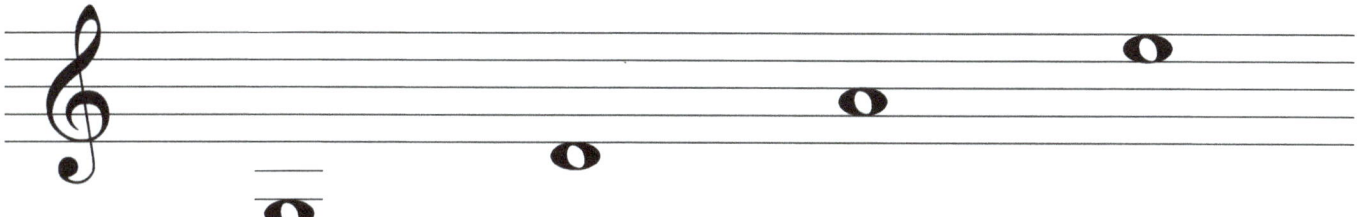

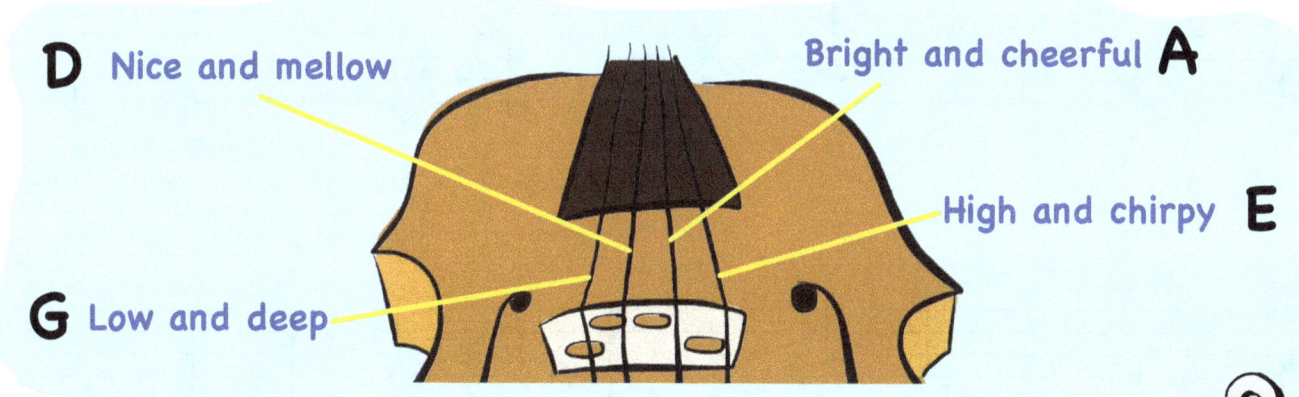

D Nice and mellow
Bright and cheerful A
High and chirpy E
G Low and deep

Which string produces the lowest/HEAVIEST sound? _____

Which string produces the highest/lightest sound? _____

Bar Lines

Bars are like classrooms. Each room has a certain amount of students.
Bar lines are like walls of the classrooms. And the double bar line is the end of the building.

Put an arrow where each song would end.

Now try and play each of these short tunes using the bow.

Reading Notes

Ledger lines are drawn the same distance away from the stave.

G — Has 2 extra line
D — Hangs on the bottom line
A — Sits in the 2nd space
E — Sits on the top space

Copy and name the notes of the open strings. (Use capital letters.)

G

D

A

E

Write the letter names of these notes for the open strings.

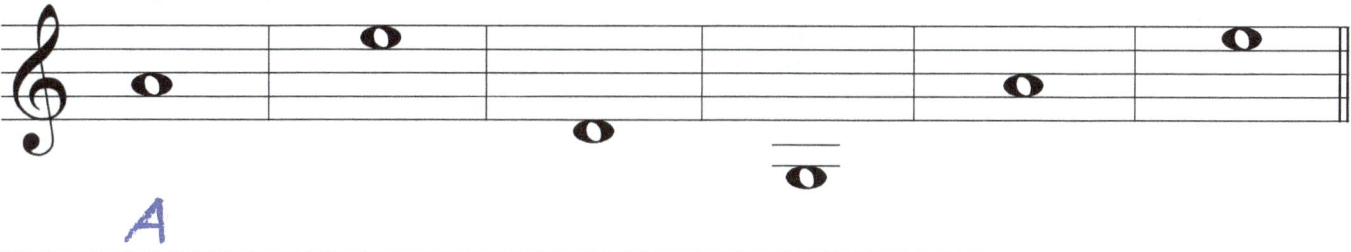

A

Draw the notes of the open strings.

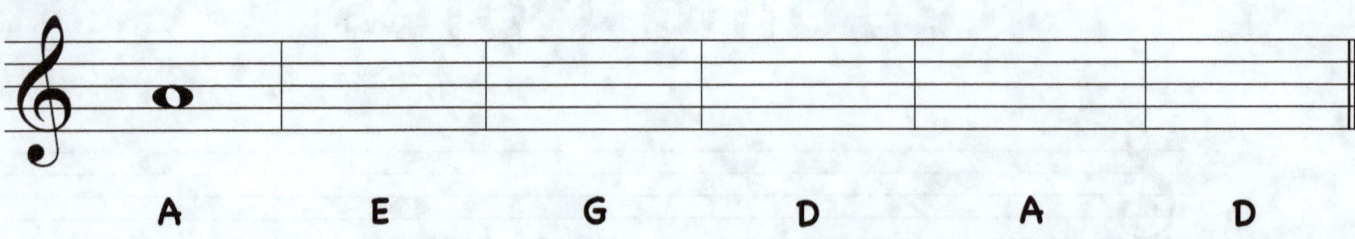

A   E   G   D   A   D

Match the notes and colour the correct open string.

There are other ways of remembering the names of your notes in between the open string notes.

How many lines does a stave have?

How many spaces does a stave have?

Below is how we would remember our notes using acronyms.

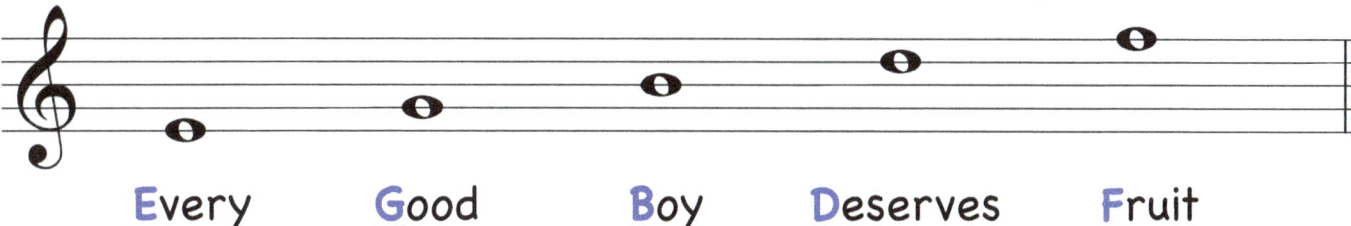

Every   Good   Boy   Deserves   Fruit

As for the notes in the spaces, all we need to do is use the alphabet which we already know and count up and down between the lines.
Let us see if you can figure out the notes in between.

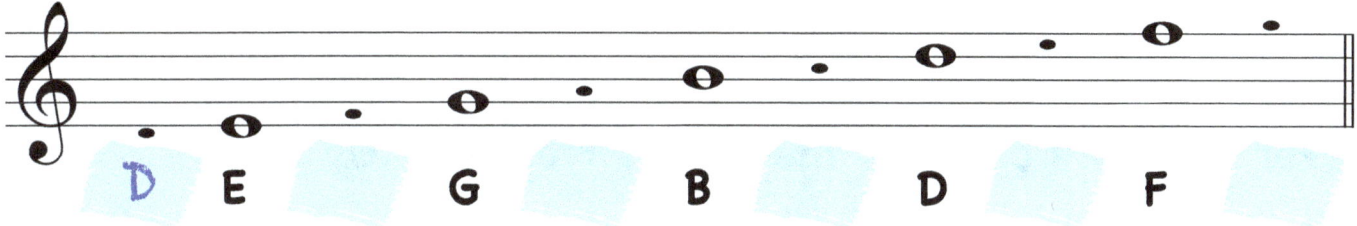

D   E   G   B   D   F

Practise saying the acronyms and see if you would be able to identify the name of the notes.

Do you remember the names of the open strings?

www.stringstastic.com

Name these notes.

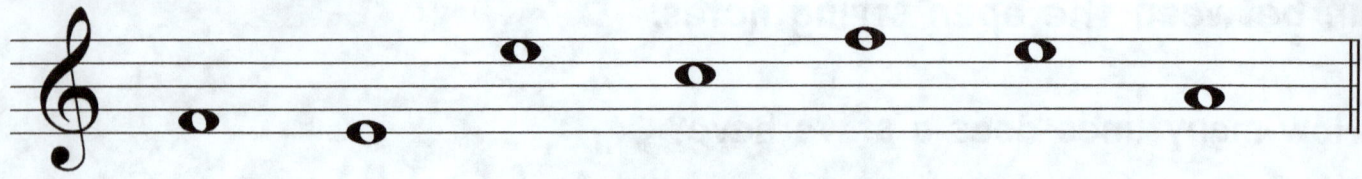

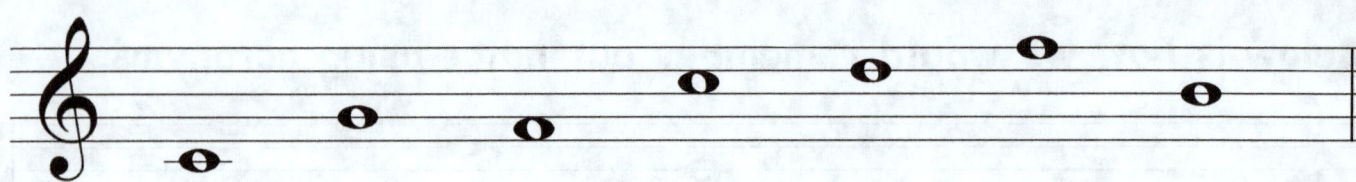

Write your alphabet from A to Z.

_____

_____

For music we only use the letters from A to G.

A   B   C   D   E   F   G

The note after G goes back to A.

See if you can memorize your alphabet backwards from G to A.

By now you should have 3 or 4 strips on your fingerboard.

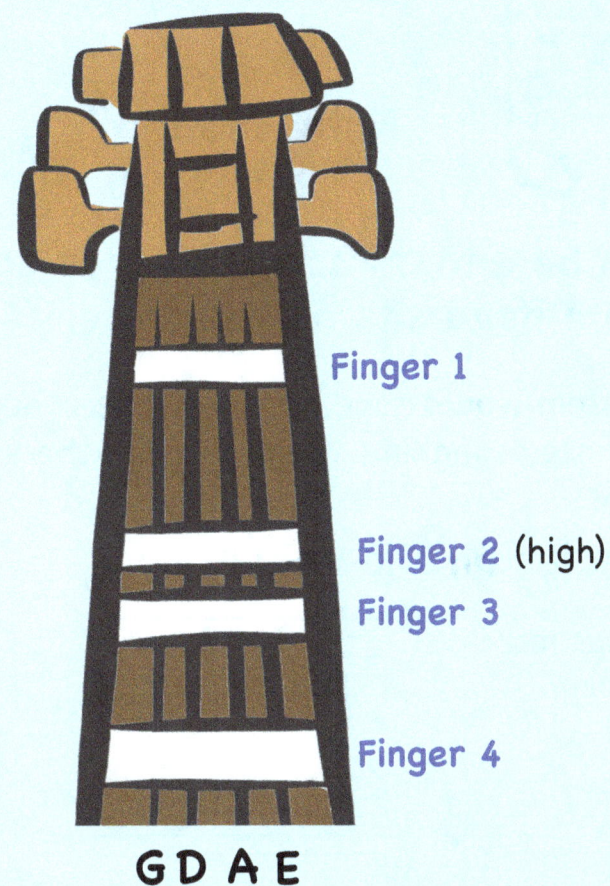

G D A E

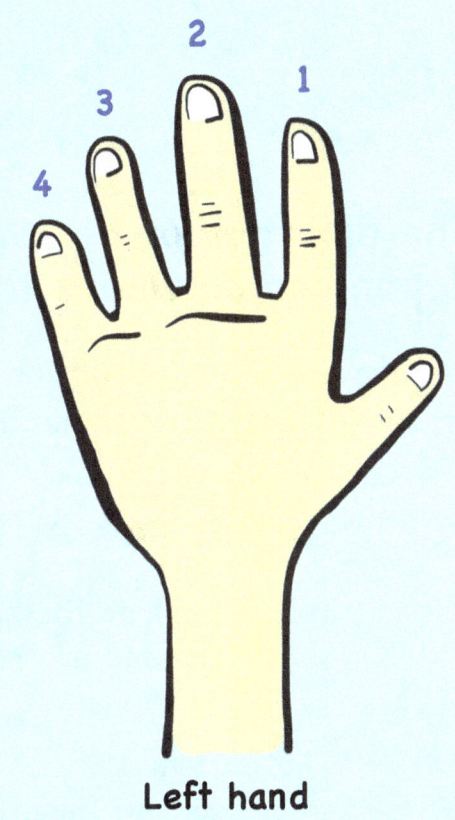

Left hand

Play all the notes of each string using all your fingers starting with the open string.

Call out each finger number while playing each note starting from open string (zero).

Printable flashcards and more work sheet on notes for individual open strings available at **www.stringstastic.com**

Position of Stems

Stem

Note Head

The direction of a stem can be either facing down or up depending on where the note head sits on the stave.

To figure out which direction the stem would face, think of the space distribution of the note heads and stems making them even on the stave.

Let us look at the notes on the middle line.

Which part of the stave has more space. The top or the bottom?

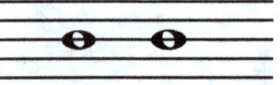

The bottom and the top part of the stave has the same amount of space.

Because of this, the stems can face either upwards or downwards.

Let us look at the notes from the middle line downwards.
(Low notes)

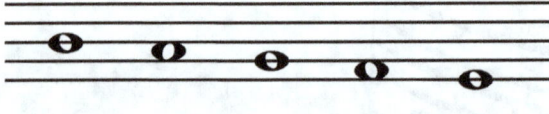

Which part of the stave has more space. The top or the bottom?

The top part of the stave has more space.

Because of this, the stems will face upwards.
Remember that the stems are drawn on the right side of the note to make the note look like the letter 'd'.

Let us look at the notes from the middle line upwards.
(High notes)

Which part of the stave has more space. The top or the bottom?

The bottom part of the stave has more space.

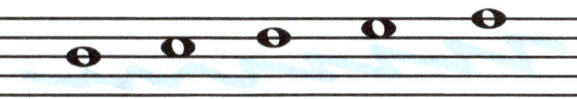

Because of this, the stems will face downwards.
Remember that the stems are drawn on the left side of the note to make the note look like a letter 'P'.

The note head is like a seed and the stem is the stick growing out. The direction of a stem can be either facing down or up depending on which part of the stave has more space.

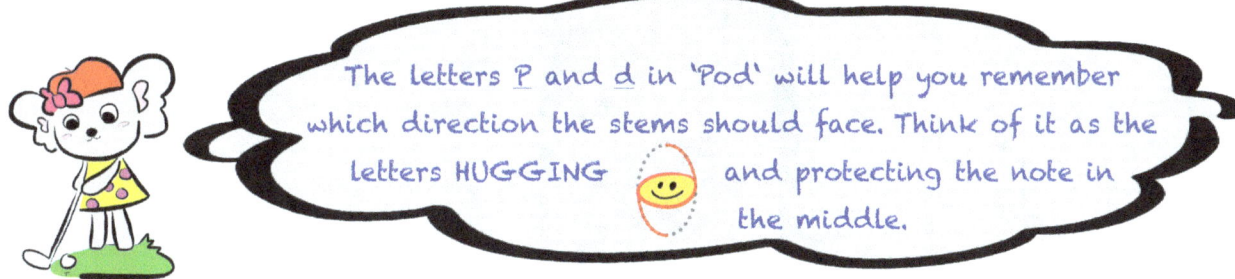

The letters P and d in 'Pod' will help you remember which direction the stems should face. Think of it as the letters HUGGING and protecting the note in the middle.

Add a stem to every note.

Now let us name the notes above.

Some stems are facing the wrong direction. Correct them so they sit properly on the stave.

Tip: "Replant" the seeds and figure out which direction they would grow.

Note Values

NOTE	NOTE VALUE	NAME
♩	1	crotchet
♪ (half note)	2	minim
♪. (dotted half)	3	dotted minim
o	4	semibreve

Draw the notes and their value.

Crotchet

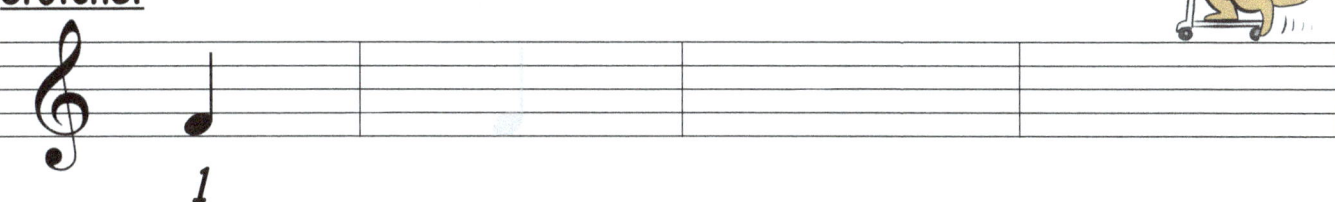
1

Minim

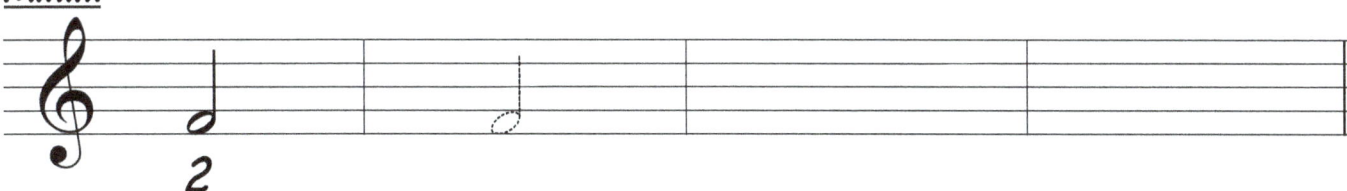
2

Dotted Minim

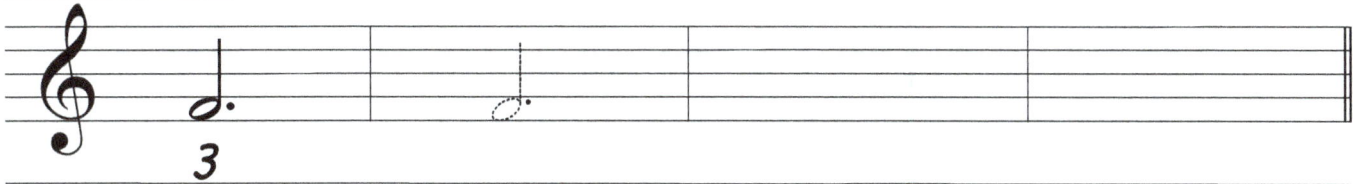
3

Semibreve

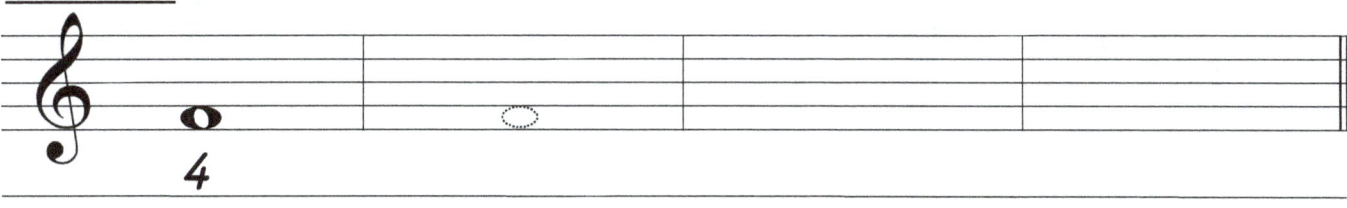
4

Write the note value of each note.

♩ 𝅝 𝅗𝅥. 𝅝 𝅗𝅥 𝅗𝅥 𝅗𝅥. ♩

1

𝅝 𝅗𝅥 𝅗𝅥. ♩ ♩ ♩ 𝅝 𝅗𝅥

Match the notes to the correct name.

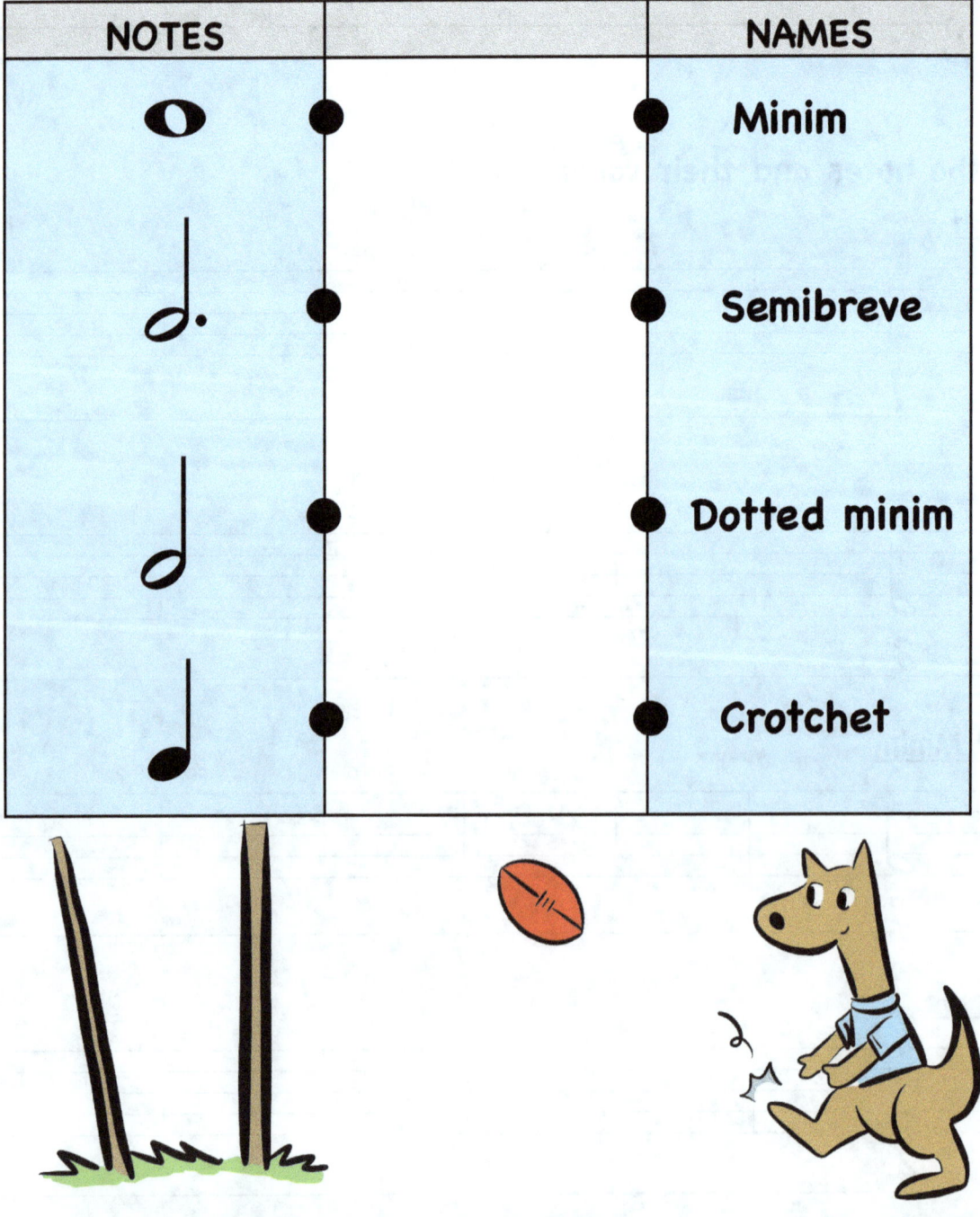

Count the number in each group. Draw the total value of each group. (Use crotchet note values.)

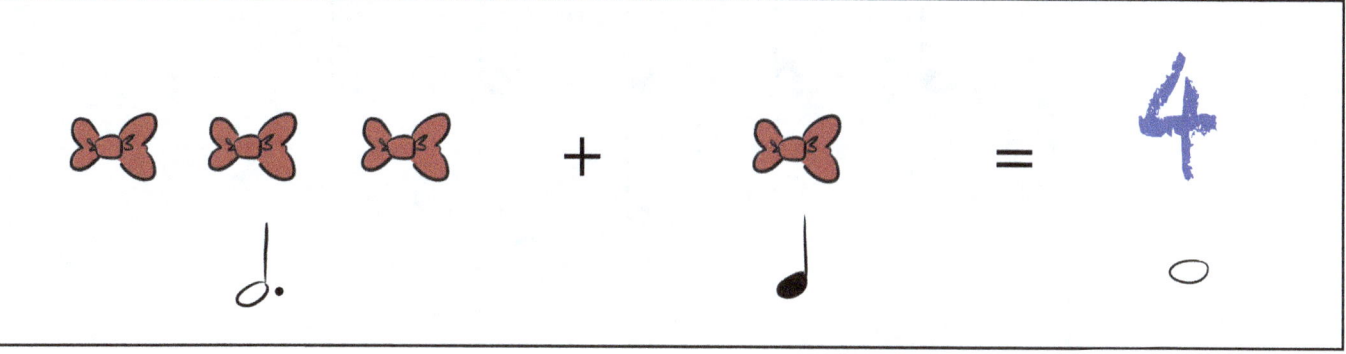

(You can draw more than one note if the value is more than 4 counts.)

Clap and count the beats.

Using the rhythms above, write your own music using the open string notes (G, D, A, E). You can write TWO different tunes on the same rhythm.

Example:

Rhythm 1

Rhythm 2

Rhythm 3

Rhythm 4

Now try and play each of your short tunes pizz.

What have we learnt so far?

1. How many strings does a violin have? Name them.

_____

2. Label and name the different parts of the violin using the words given.

| bridge |
| chin rest |
| end button |
| f holes |
| fine tuning |
| fingerboard |
| frog |
| horse hair |
| pegs |
| scroll |
| tail piece |

3. Fill in the blanks.

SYMBOL	NAME
𝄞	
	stave
▱	
♩↙	

SYMBOL	NAME	COUNT
	semibreve	
♪		
♩		
		3

www.stringstastic.com

4. Mark the correct string on the violin.

Eg.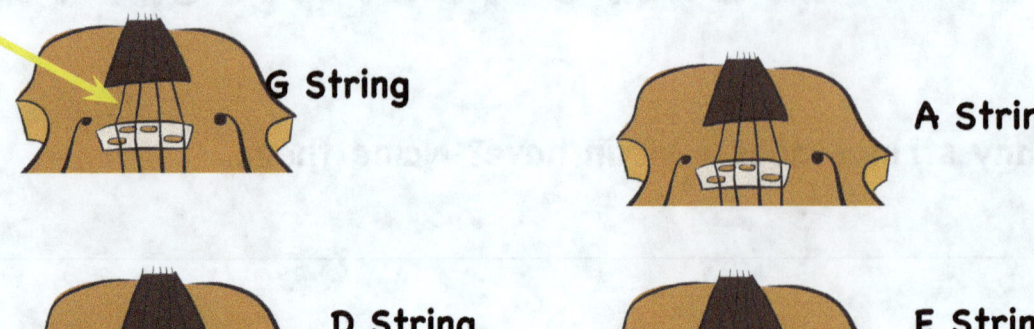

G String   A String

D String   E String

5. Draw and name these notes on the open string in semibreves.

Eg.

  D   A   ___

  G   D   ___

  E   ___   ___

6. What letter note comes after G in music?

Rests

NOTE	REST		NOTE VALUE
♩	𝄽	If you straighten this wavy line, it looks like the number 1	1
𝅗𝅥	▃	Hat closed half full	2
𝅝	▀	You can fill more things with the hat open	4

▀ may also be used as a whole bar rest.

Copy each rest and count them.

Crotchet rest (lightning/slanted ≳ + capital C)

1   1

Minim rest (sitting on 3rd line)

1 2   1 2

Semibreve rest (hanging on 4th line)

1 2 3 4   1 2 3 4

Write down the value of each rest.

The sea creatures in Atlantic City live in their own luxurious underwater apartment. Help them find their correct place.

Time Signature

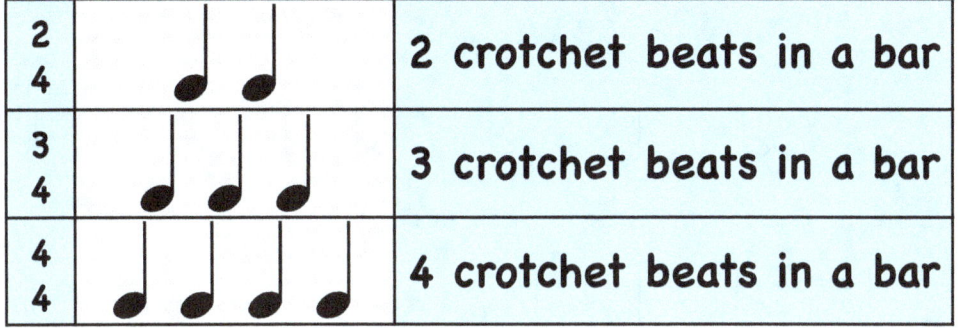
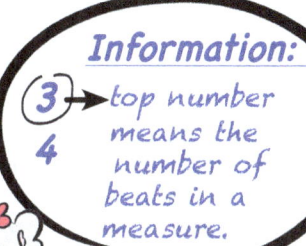

Information: top number means the number of beats in a measure.

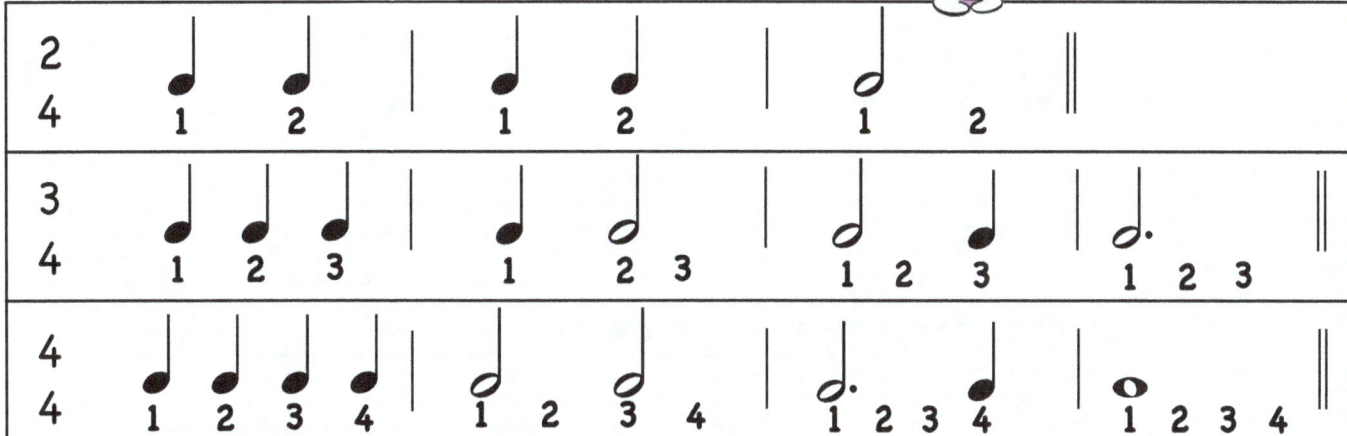

Write in the beats of each bar.

www.stringstastic.com

Write in the correct beats and time signature.

Put in the bar lines and write in the beats.

Write in the beats for each of these bars.

1 2 3 4   1 2 3 4   1 2 3 4   1 2 3 4

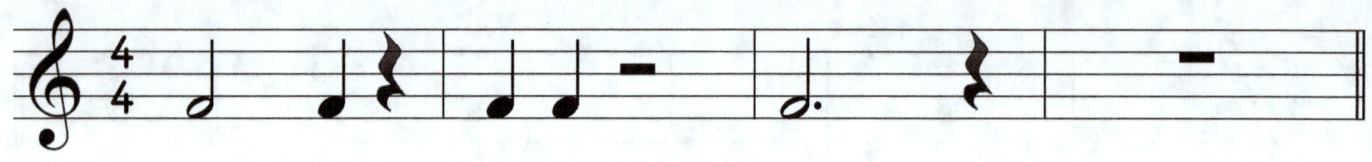

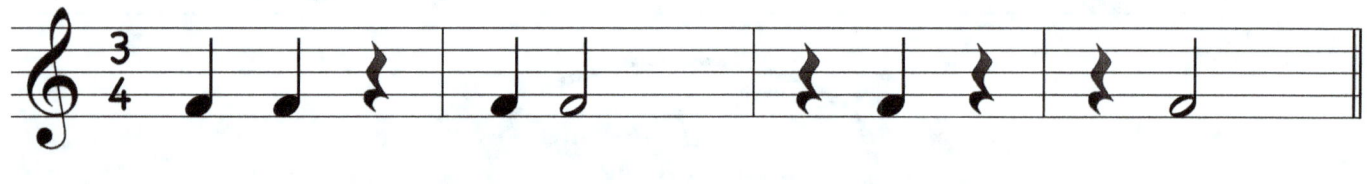

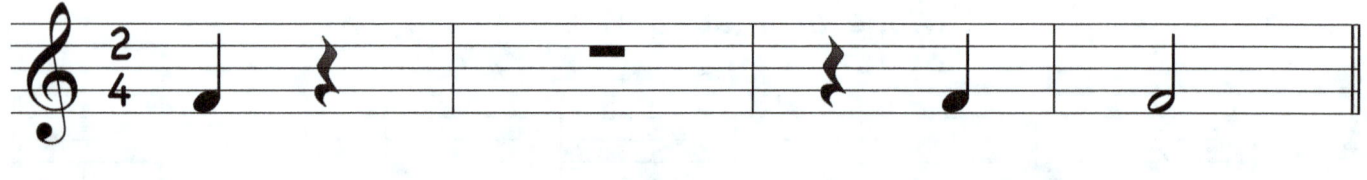

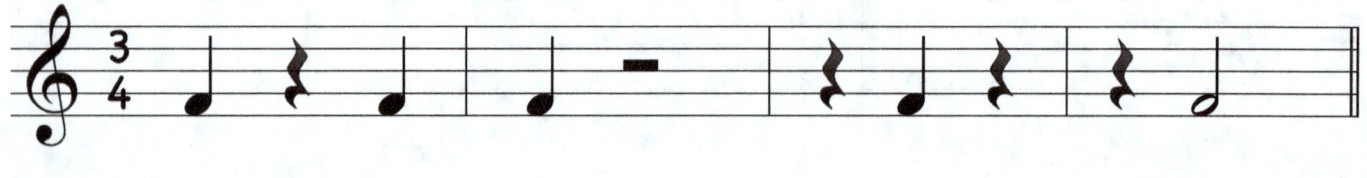

Accidentals

♭ Flat (Lower)	♮ Natural (Normal = no change)	♯ Sharp (Higher)

♯ **Sharp** ↑ = raises a note by 1 step
(raises the finger by 1 step)

♭ **Flat** ↓ = lowers a note by 1 step
(lowers the finger by 1 step)

♮ **Natural** = puts a note back to its original pitch

In order, arrange the accidental from highest to lowest and name the accidentals.

ACCIDENTALS	NAME
♯	

The sharp sign should be drawn on the same space or line as the note head.

CORRECT   WRONG   WRONG

Trace the sharp signs below and draw THREE more through any line and THREE more in any space.

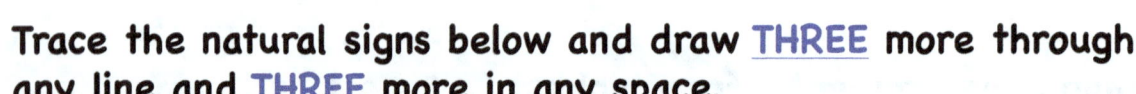

Trace the flat signs below and draw THREE more through any line and THREE more in any space.

Trace the natural signs below and draw THREE more through any line and THREE more in any space.

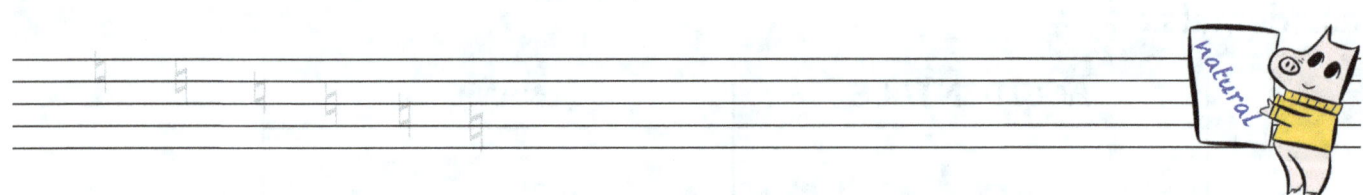

These signs are always drawn before the note head. However, when labelling a note the accidental signs are written after the note.

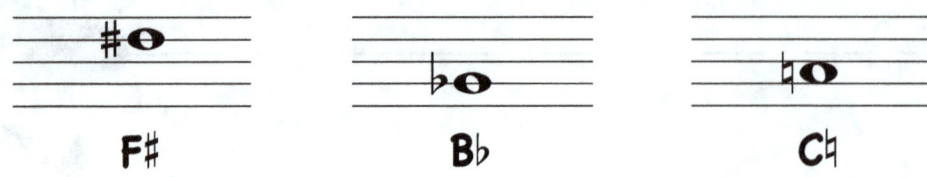

F♯   B♭   C♮

Put a sharp (#) before every note.

Put a flat (♭) before every note.

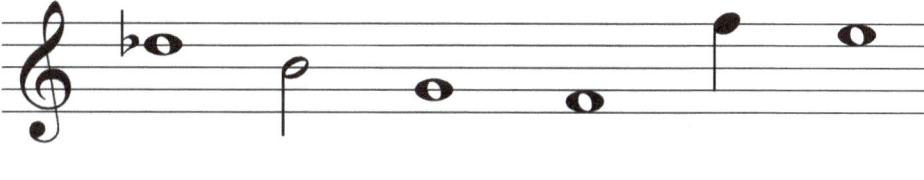

Now name the notes above.

Name the notes below.

G#

D String

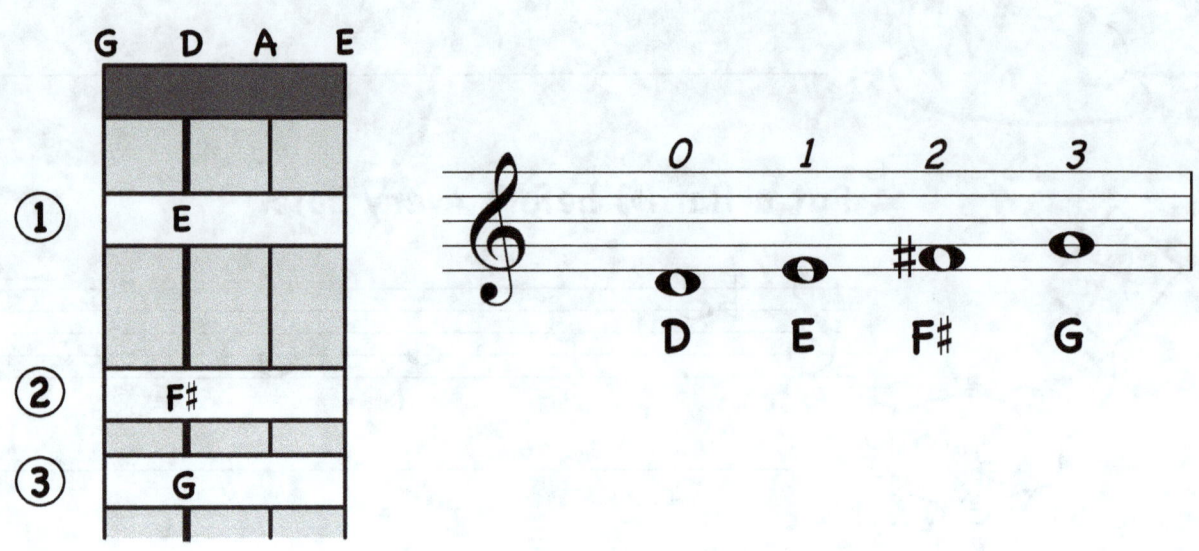

Copy each note below and their fingering accordingly.

Name the notes and their fingering accordingly.

Two children went to the pet shop. Each tries to touch the animals with their finger. Colour the animals according to the finger they used.

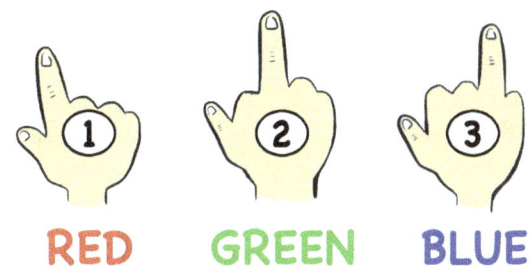

RED   GREEN   BLUE

Strings and Note Names

Remember the letters you use in music to name the music notes? What are they? _____

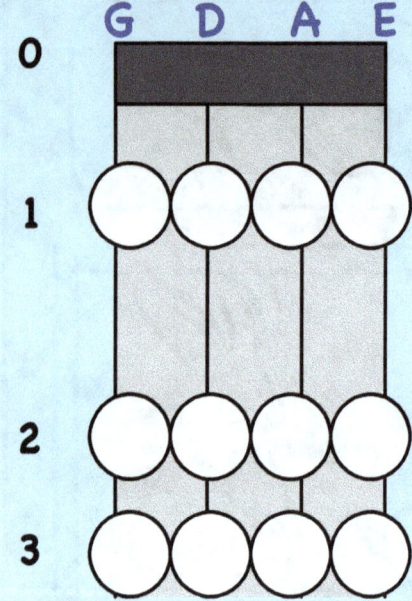

Name each fingering on the violin according to your music alphabet.

The open strings are already given.

Make sure that there is a SHARP on the 2nd finger on the D and A string.

Which finger tab has no sharps? _____

Pluck each note on your violin while saying the letter names of each note starting on the open G string.

Now try playing and naming each note backwards starting on finger 3 on the E string.

A String

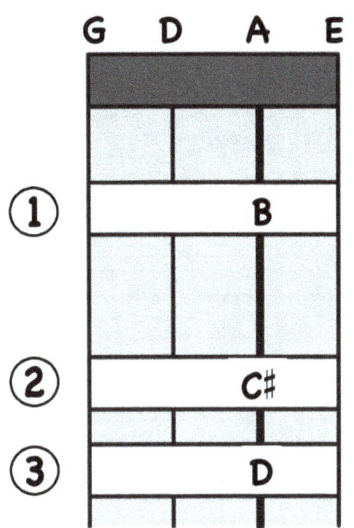
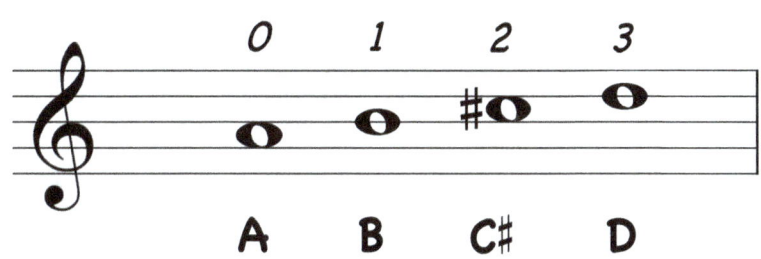

Copy each note below and their fingering accordingly.

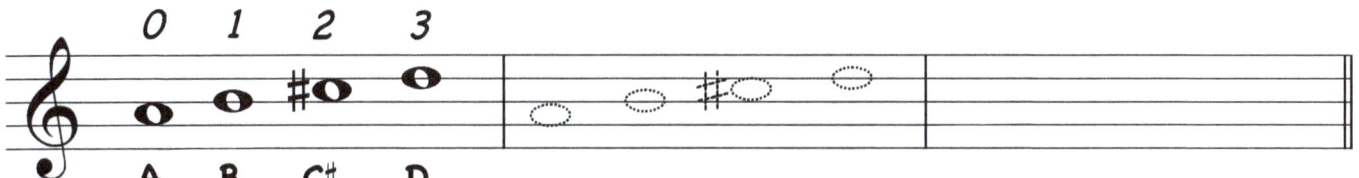

Fill in the blanks.

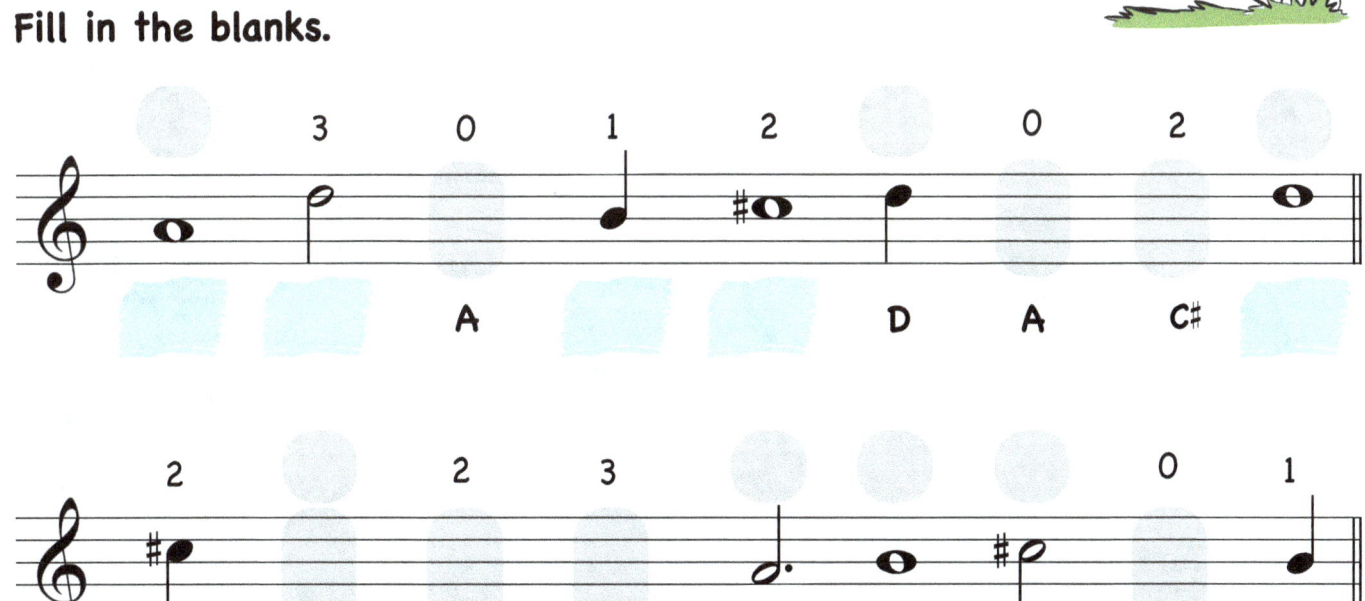

Draw the notes of these fingering on the A string and name the notes.

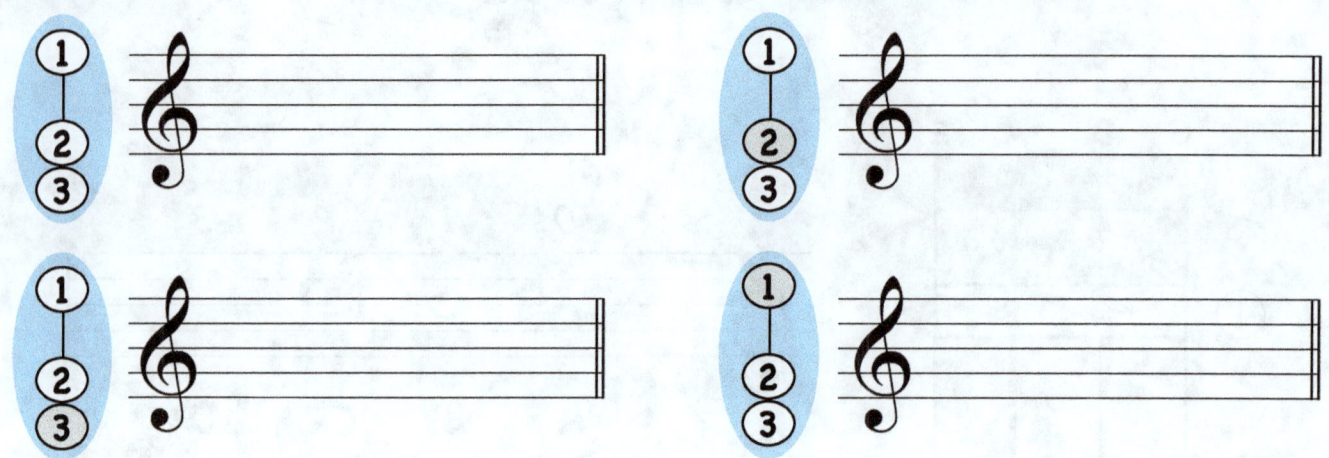

Tommy and his friends all finish their music lessons at the same time. Who reaches home 1st?

Pete the Pig:

Max the Turtle:

Tommy the Kangaroo:

Kate the Penguin:

Revision D and A Strings

In semibreves, draw the notes as shown, including the open string notes.

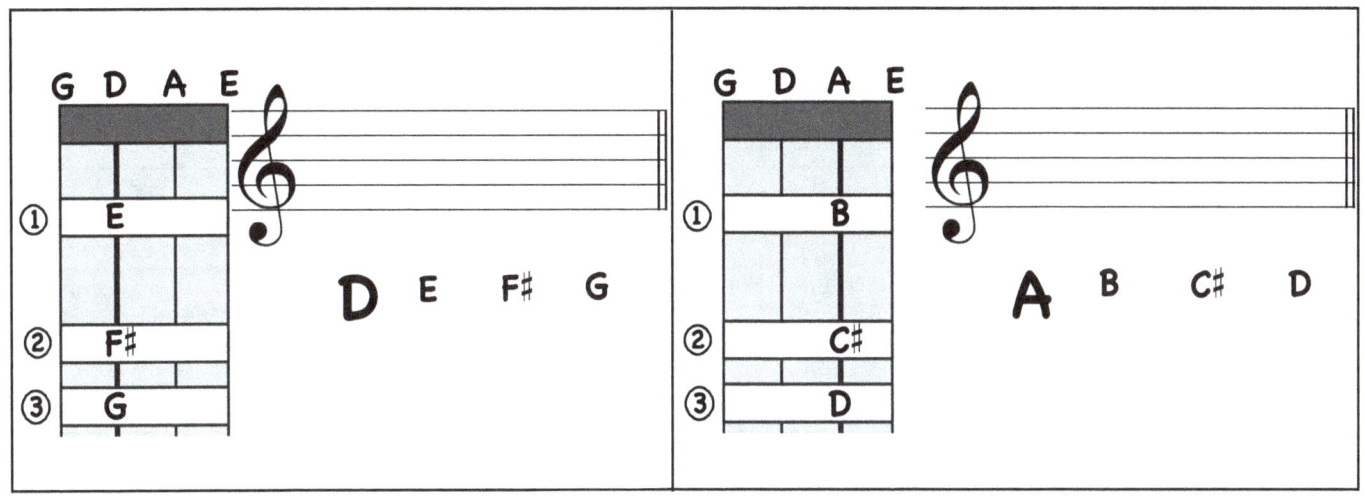

Which fingering do you use on these notes?

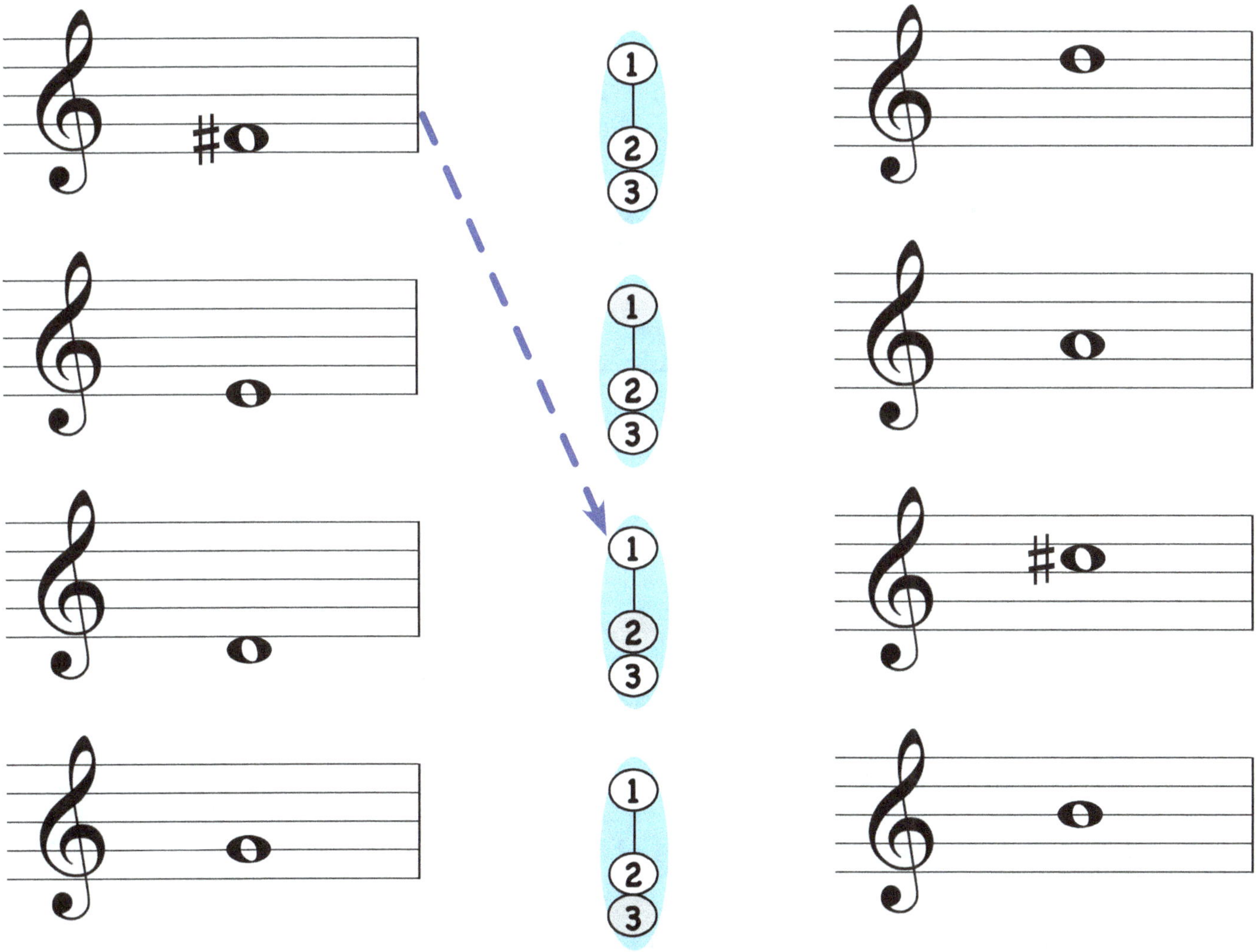

Name each note according to the fingering and label it on the string.

STRINGS	FINGERING	NAME OF THE NOTE
A string	3	D
D string		G
A string	1	
D string	2	
D string		E
A string		A

G String

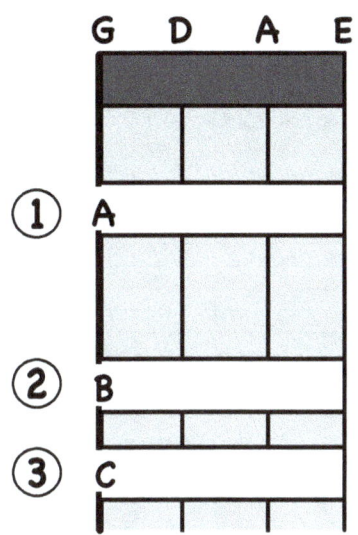
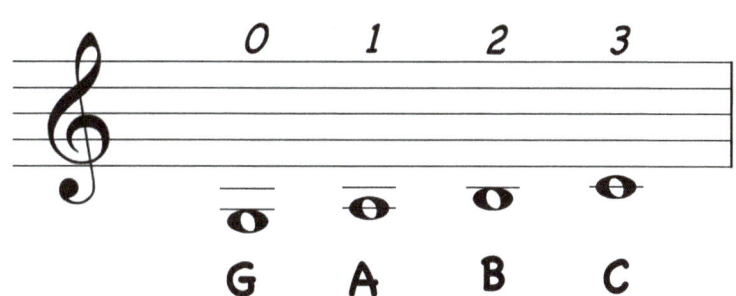

Copy these notes and notice how many ledger lines they have.

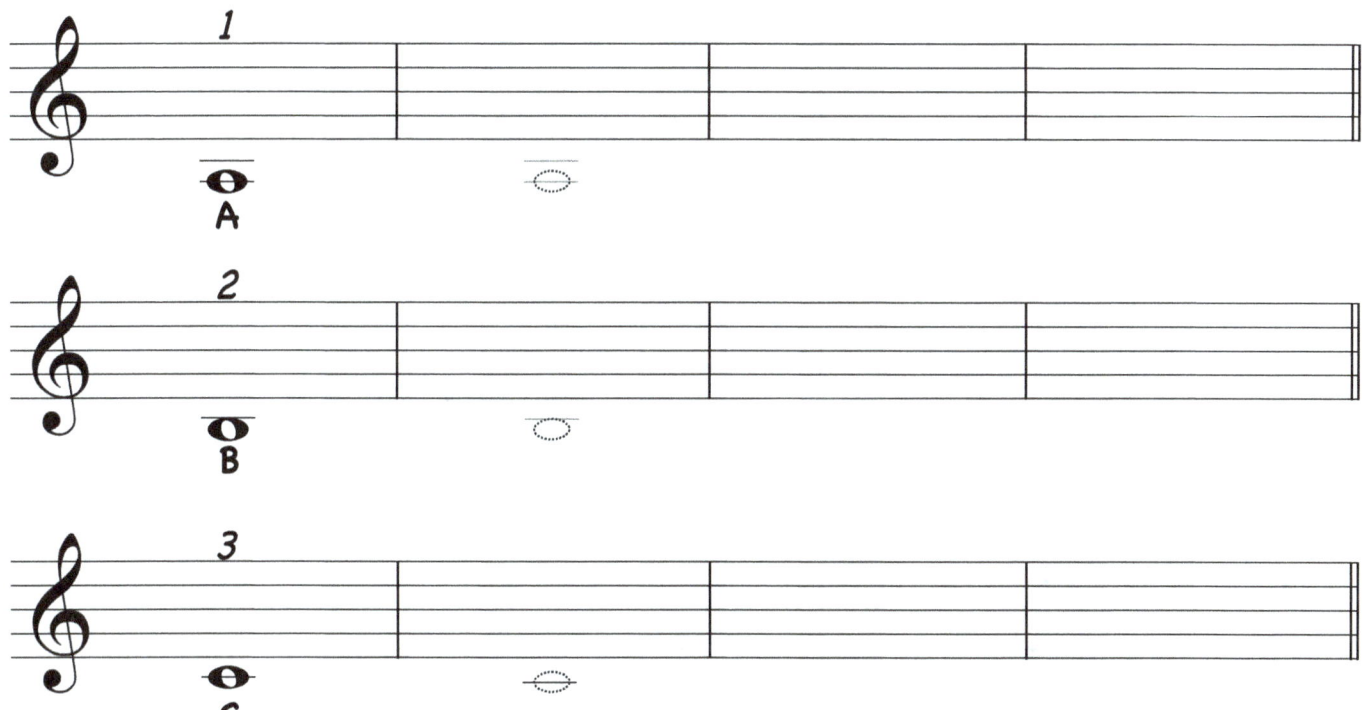

Draw the notes of these fingerings and name the notes on the G string.

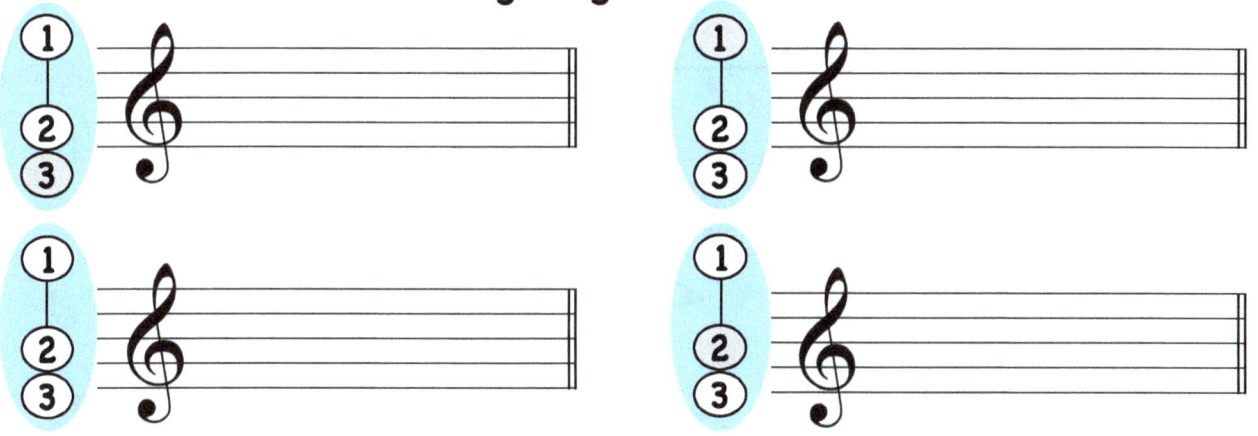

Which fingers are used to play these notes?

Colour the fingering and name the note.

C

Name the notes.

G

E String

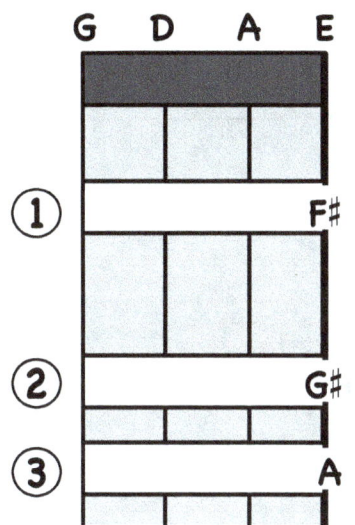

Copy each note below and their fingering accordingly.

Now play these notes on the violin while naming them aloud.

Name the notes and its fingering.

Match the fingering on these notes.

Revision (on all strings)

1. Draw all the open string notes according to the name given.

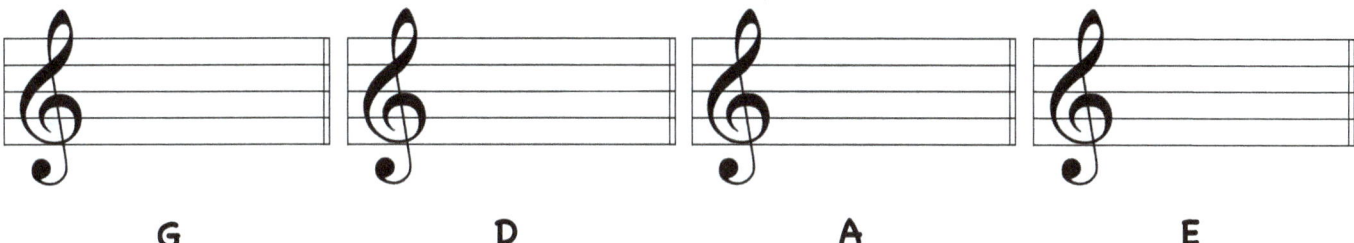

G   D   A   E

2. Name the string where each of these notes are found.

① ② ③	G	D String	① ② ③	A	
① ② ③	E		① ② ③	F♯	
① ② ③	C		① ② ③	E	
① ② ③	C♯		① ② ③	D	
① ② ③	A		① ② ③	F♯	

3. Write down the fingering and name the notes.

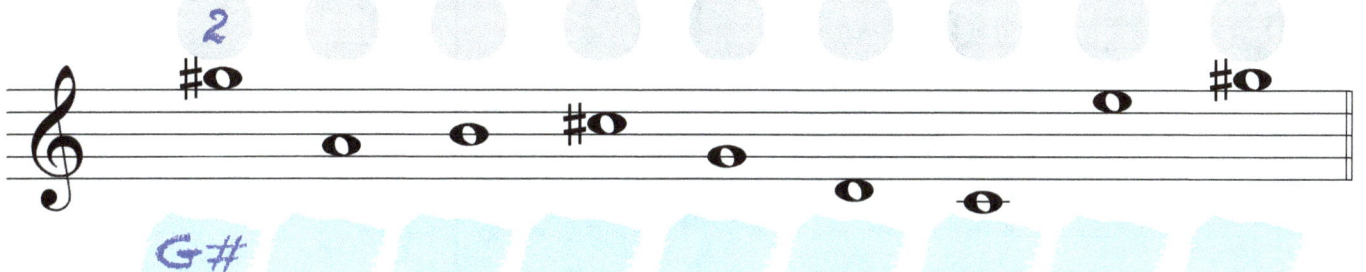

G♯

4. Draw these notes on the stave.

(note drawn)	E
	F#
	F
	G
	C#
	E
	D
	A

5. Draw 2 different notes and colour in their fingering.

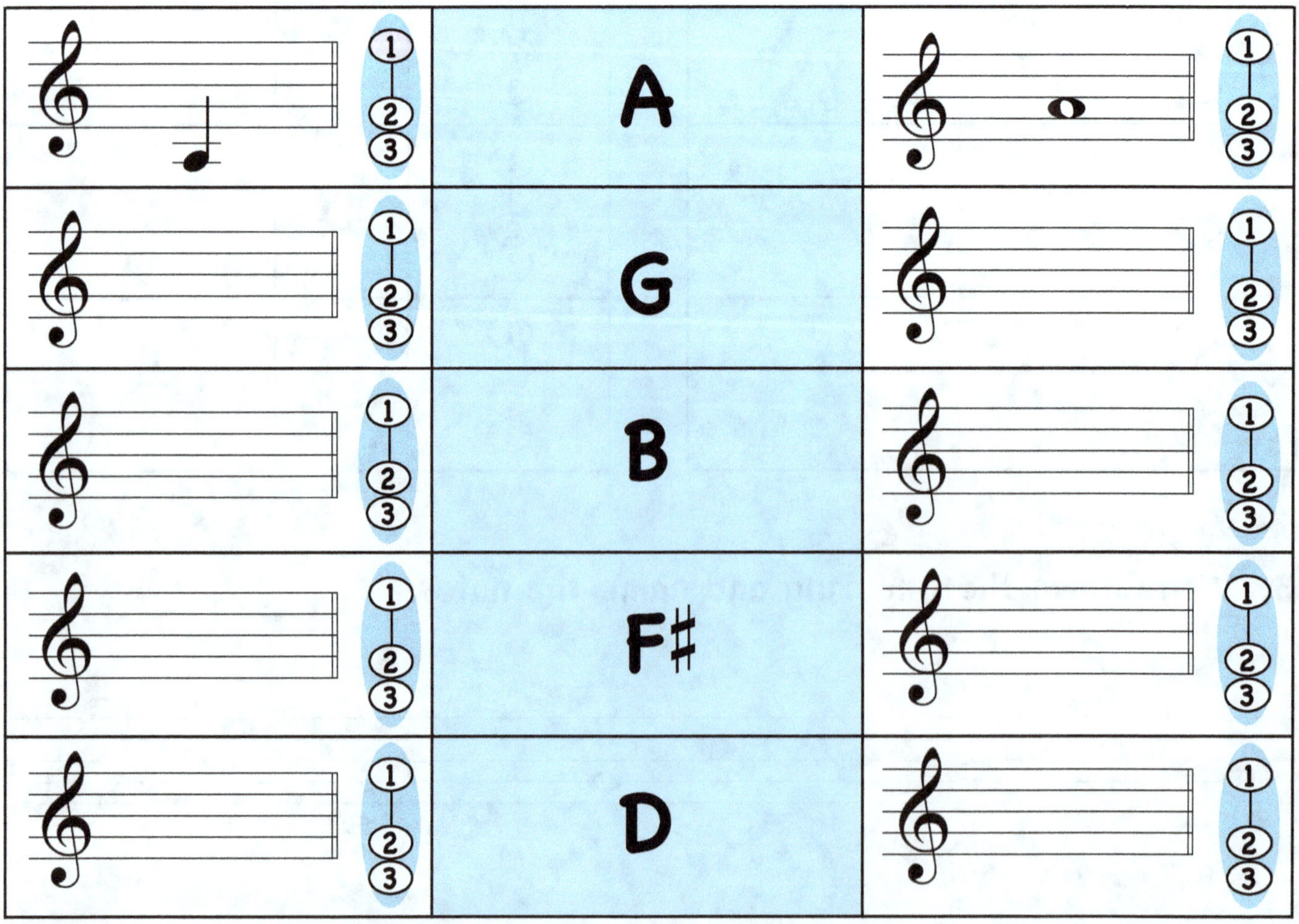

Stave & fingering	Note	Stave & fingering
(quarter note drawn)	A	(whole note drawn)
	G	
	B	
	F#	
	D	

Name: _____ Date: _____

Test

TOTAL MARKS: _____/100

1. Name these notes. _____/12

2. Label above each note in question 1 with the correct fingering.
   (0, 1, 2, 3) _____/12

3. How many beats are these notes? _____/12

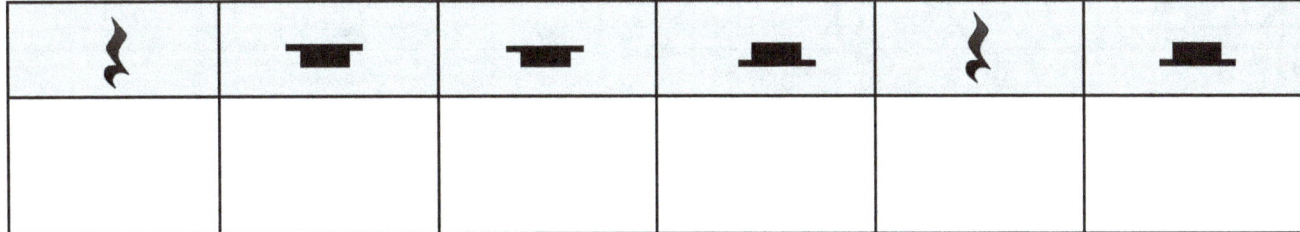

4. How many beats are these rests? _____/12

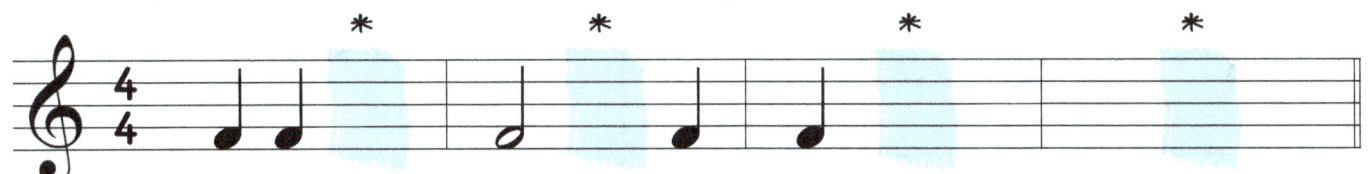

5. Complete each bar with one missing note. _____/8

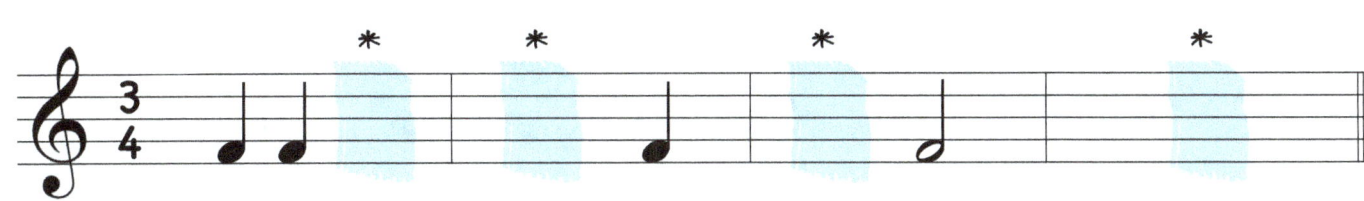

6. **Complete each bar with one missing rest.** ___/8

7. **Write the beats and the time signature.** 2/4 3/4 4/4   ___/20

8. **Fill in the two different fingerings for these notes and indicate the string they are on.** ___/16

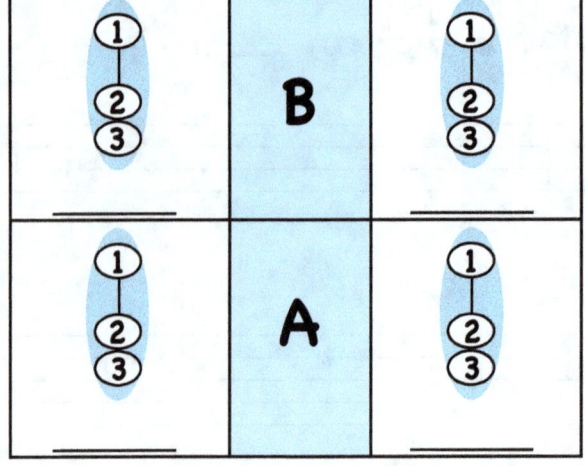

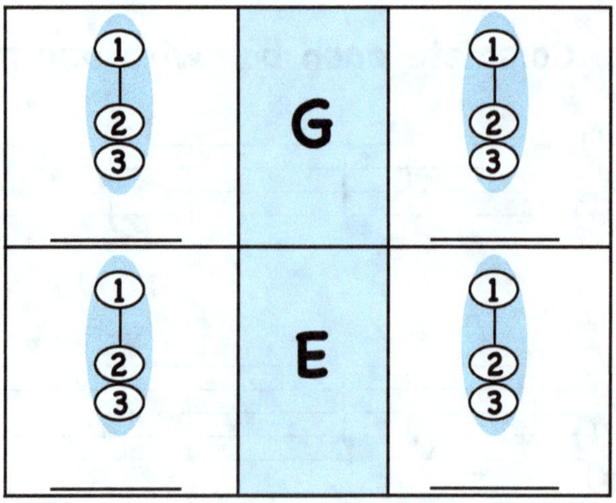

STRINGSTASTIC

Lorraine is a multitalented instrumentalist and international educator who loves finding new and exciting ways for students to learn the violin. Along her musical journey and exposure to the various educational methods including Kodaly, Suzuki, Orff, Dalcroze, and Alexander Technique, Lorraine has found that she can integrate these various methods into her own teaching technique for the benefit of her students. Lorraine's passion for music and education is shown in her STRINGSTASTIC book series which will inspire young players to excel and develop to their full potential.

STRINGSTASTIC MINI

Specifically suited for children aged 4 to 7, these two books present music theory using fun exercises, colourful illustrations and stickers for the exercises. Young players will derive much pleasure in learning music from these books.

STRINGSTASTIC ENSEMBLE
violin, viola and cello

Specifically suited for children aged 6 to 10, these three books contain colourful illustrations, exciting written exercises and graphics which are interesting to the child.

STRINGSTASTIC GRADED

Specifically suited for students of all ages who are quick learners or who are interested in successfully completing music theory exams.

Design & illustration by MeiDesign

www.stringstastic.com

ISBN 978-0-9954128-0-4